Affirmations of The United Methodist Church

Beliefs and Convictions of
The United Methodist Church
From *THE BOOK OF DISCIPLINE*

Approved by The 1996 General Conference

DISCIPLESHIP RESOURCES

P.O. BOX 840 • NASHVILLE, TENNESSEE 37202-0840

www.discipleshipresources.org

ISBN 0-88177-255-0

Quotations are from *The Book of Discipline of The United Methodist Church, 1996*. Copyright © 1996 The United Methodist Publishing House. All rights reserved. Used by permission.

AFFIRMATIONS OF THE UNITED METHODIST CHURCH. Copyright © 1998 by Discipleship Resources. All rights reserved. Printed in the United States of America. No part of this book may be reproduced in any manner whatsoever, print or electronic, without written permission, except in the case of brief quotations embodied in critical articles or reviews. For information regarding rights and permissions, contact Discipleship Resources Editorial Offices, P. O. Box 840, Nashville, TN 37202-0840, phone (615) 340-7068, fax (615) 340-1789, e-mail mgregory@gbod.org.

DR255

Contents

Introduction

The Book of Discipline of The United
Methodist Church provides the legislative
framework for the work of the denomination. The majority of the contents of The
Book of Discipline describes the rules and
regulations that govern the organization
and operation of the annual, jurisdictional,
and general conferences, as well as the
local churches, districts, and general
agencies. The Book of Discipline also contains
those provisions that regulate lay membership in local churches, ministerial relationships to the annual conferences, issues
relating to property, and various judicial
processes.

The historic title for this book was
The Doctrines and Discipline of The Methodist
Episcopal Church. This title was used by the
predecessor Methodist denominations
until the 1968 merger of three Methodist
bodies.

But the former title does indicate that,
along with all of the rules and regulations,

The Book of Discipline contains many beliefs and affirmations of The United Methodist Church.

Contained in *The Book of Discipline* are three historical statements of belief and doctrine: The Articles of Religion of The Methodist Church, The General Rule of The Methodist Church, and the Confession of Faith of the Evangelical United Brethren Church. The first two of these were protected from modification by two Restrictive Rules passed in 1808. The third is protected from modification from the initial 1963 statement by a third Restrictive Rule. These Restrictive Rules were made a part of The Constitution of The United Methodist Church (Articles 16 and 19) at the time of its creation in 1968. Therefore, "the General Conference shall not revoke, alter, or change . . ." these three doctrinal statements.

However, in addition to these three key documents, *The Book of Discipline* contains many other expressions of belief or conviction of The United Methodist Church. These affirmations have been brought before the delegates to the General Conference and have been debated and approved. Those presented in the 1996 edition of *The Book of Discipline* represent the position of the 1996 General Conference.

This booklet gathers together many of these affirmations concerning the life and ministry of The United Methodist Church. These have been subject to quadrennial review and many have been modified from time to time to reflect the current thinking of the denomination. (None of the statements included in this booklet have been taken from the three protected doctrinal statements cited above.)

In reading through these statements United Methodists can note key affirmations of the church and understand more clearly those convictions that shape the life and ministry of the denomination. These statements speak to the essential beliefs of The United Methodist Church today.

The Constitution

The Church as a Community of True Believers
(The Constitution of The United Methodist Church, Preamble, page 21)

The church is a community of all true believers under the Lordship of Christ. It is the redeemed and redeeming fellowship in which the Word of God is preached by persons divinely called, and the sacraments are duly administered according to Christ's own appointment. Under the discipline of the Holy Spirit the church seeks to provide for the maintenance of worship, the edification of believers, and the redemption of the world.

The Inclusiveness of the Church
(The Constitution of The United Methodist Church, Article IV, Para. 4, page 22)

The United Methodist Church is a part of the church universal, which is one

Body in Christ. Therefore all persons, without regard to race, color, national origin, status, or economic condition, shall be eligible to attend its worship services, to participate in its programs, and, when they take the appropriate vows, to be admitted into its membership in any local church in the connection. In The United Methodist Church no conference or other organizational unit of the Church shall be structured so as to exclude any member or any constituent body of the Church because of race, color, national origin, status, or economic condition.

Our Doctrinal Heritage

**United Methodists Profess
the Historic Christian Faith in God**
*(Doctrinal Standards and Our Theological Task,
Section 1 — Our Doctrinal Heritage, Para. 60,
page 39)*

United Methodists profess the historic Christian faith in God, incarnate in Jesus Christ for our salvation and ever at work in human history in the Holy Spirit. Living in a covenant of grace under the Lordship of Jesus Christ, we participate in the first fruits of God's coming reign and pray in hope for its full realization on earth as in heaven.

Our heritage in doctrine and our present theological task focus upon a renewed grasp of the sovereignty of God and of God's love in Christ amid the continuing crises of human existence.

Our forebears in the faith reaffirmed the ancient Christian message as found in the apostolic witness even as they applied

3

it anew in their own circumstances.

Their preaching and teaching were grounded in Scripture, informed by Christian tradition, enlivened in experience, and tested by reason.

Their labors inspire and inform our attempts to convey the saving gospel to our world with its needs and aspirations.

Basic Christian Affirmations

(Doctrinal Standards and Our Theological Task, Section 1 – Our Doctrinal Heritage, Para. 60, pages 41-42)

With Christians of other communions we confess belief in the triune God—Father, Son, and Holy Spirit. This confession embraces the biblical witness to God's activity in creation, encompasses God's gracious self-involvement in the dramas of history, and anticipates the consummation of God's reign.

The created order is designed for the well-being of all creatures and as the place of human dwelling in covenant with God. As sinful creatures, however, we have broken that covenant, become estranged from God, wounded ourselves and one another, and wreaked havoc throughout the natural order. We stand in need of redemption.

We hold in common with all Christians a faith in the mystery of salvation in and through Jesus Christ. At the heart of the gospel of salvation is God's incarnation in Jesus of Nazareth. Scripture witnesses to the redeeming love of God in Jesus' life and teachings, his atoning death, his resurrection, his sovereign presence in history, his triumph over the powers of evil and death, and his promised return. Because God truly loves us in spite of our willful sin, God judges us, summons us to repentance, pardons us, receives us by that grace given to us in Jesus Christ, and gives us hope of life eternal.

We share the Christian belief that God's redemptive love is realized in human life by the activity of the Holy Spirit, both in personal experience and in the community of believers. This community is the church, which the Spirit has brought into existence for the healing of the nations.

Through faith in Jesus Christ we are forgiven, reconciled to God, and transformed as people of the new covenant.

"Life in the Spirit" involves diligent use of the means of grace such as praying, fasting, attending upon the sacraments, and inward searching in solitude. It also encompasses the communal life of the church in worship, mission, evangelism, service, and social witness.

We understand ourselves to be part of Christ's universal church when by adoration, proclamation, and service we become conformed to Christ. We are initiated and incorporated into this community of faith by Baptism, receiving the promise of the Spirit that re-creates and transforms us. Through the regular celebration of Holy Communion, we participate in the risen presence of Jesus Christ and are thereby nourished for faithful discipleship.

We pray and work for the coming of God's realm and reign to the world and rejoice in the promise of everlasting life that overcomes death and the forces of evil.

With other Christians we recognize that the reign of God is both a present and future reality. The church is called to be that place where the first signs of the reign of God are identified and acknowledged in the world. Wherever persons are being made new creatures in Christ, wherever the insights and resources of the gospel are brought to bear on the life of the world, God's reign is already effective in its healing and renewing power.

We also look to the end time in which God's work will be fulfilled. This prospect gives us hope in our present actions as individuals and as the Church. This expectation saves us from resignation and motivates our continuing witness and service.

We share with many Christian communions a recognition of the authority of Scripture in matters of faith, the confession that our justification as sinners is by grace through faith, and the sober realization that the Church is in need of continual reformation and renewal.

We affirm the general ministry of all baptized Christians who share responsibility for building up the church and reaching out in mission and service to the world.

With other Christians, we declare the essential oneness of the Church in Christ Jesus. This rich heritage of shared Christian belief finds expression in our hymnody and liturgies. Our unity is affirmed in the historic creeds as we confess one holy, catholic, and apostolic Church. It is also experienced in joint ventures of ministry and in various forms of ecumenical cooperation.

Nourished by common roots of this shared Christian heritage, the branches of Christ's church have developed diverse traditions that enlarge our store of shared understandings. Our avowed ecumenical commitment as United Methodists is to gather our own doctrinal emphases into the larger Christian unity, there to be made more meaningful in a richer whole.

If we are to offer our best gifts to the common Christian treasury, we must make a deliberate effort as a church to strive for critical self-understanding. It is as Christians involved in ecumenical partnership that we embrace and examine our distinctive heritage.

Our Distinctive Heritage as United Methodists

*(Doctrinal Standards and Our Theological Task,
Section 1 – Our Doctrinal Heritage, Para 60,
page 43)*

The underlying energy of the
Wesleyan theological heritage stems from
an emphasis upon practical divinity, the
implementation of genuine Christianity
in the lives of believers.

Methodism did not arise in response to
a specific doctrinal dispute, though there
was no lack of theological controversy.
Early Methodists claimed to preach the
scriptural doctrines of the Church of
England as contained in the Articles of
Religion, the Homilies, and the *Book of
Common Prayer.*

Their task was not to formulate doctrine. Their tasks were to summon people
to experience the justifying and sanctifying grace of God and encourage people
to grow in the knowledge and love of
God through the personal and corporate
disciplines of the Christian life.

The thrust of the Wesleyan movement
and of the United Brethren and Evangeli-

cal Association was "to reform the nation, particularly the Church, and to spread scriptural holiness over the land."

Wesley's orientation toward the practical is evident in his focus upon the "scripture way of salvation." He considered doctrinal matters primarily in terms of their significance for Christian discipleship.

The Wesleyan emphasis upon the Christian life – faith and love put into practice — has been the hallmark of those traditions now incorporated into The United Methodist Church. The distinctive shape of the Wesleyan theological heritage can be seen in a constellation of doctrinal emphases that display the creating, redeeming, and sanctifying activity of God.

Distinctive Wesleyan Emphases
(Doctrinal Standards and Our Theological Task, Section 1. – Our Doctrinal Heritage, Para. 60, pages 43-46)

Although Wesley shared with many other Christians a belief in grace, justification, assurance, and sanctification, he combined them in a powerful manner to create distinctive emphases for living the full Christian life. The Evangelical United Brethren tradition, particularly as expressed by Phillip William Otterbein from a Reformed background, gave similar distinctive emphases.

Grace pervades our understanding of Christian faith and life. By grace we mean the undeserved, unmerited, and loving action of God in human existence through the ever-present Holy Spirit. While the grace of God is undivided, it precedes salvation as "prevenient grace," continues in "justifying grace," and is brought to fruition in "sanctifying grace."

We assert that God's grace is manifest in all creation even though suffering, violence, and evil are everywhere present. The goodness of creation is fulfilled in human beings, who are called to covenant partnership with God. God has endowed us with dignity and freedom and has summoned us to responsibility for our lives and the life of the world.

In God's self-revelation, Jesus Christ, we see the splendor of our true humanity. Even our sin, with its destructive consequences for all creation, does not alter God's intention for us—holiness and

11

happiness of heart. Nor does it diminish our accountability for the way we live.

Despite our brokenness, we remain creatures brought into being by a just and merciful God. The restoration of God's image in our lives requires divine grace to renew our fallen nature.

Prevenient Grace—We acknowledge God's prevenient grace, the divine love that surrounds all humanity and precedes any and all of our conscious impulses. This grace prompts our first wish to please God, our first glimmer of understanding concerning God's will, and our "first slight transient conviction" of having sinned against God.

God's grace also awakens in us an earnest longing for deliverance from sin and death and moves us toward repentance and faith.

Justification and Assurance—We believe God reaches out to the repentant believer in justifying grace with accepting and pardoning love. Wesleyan theology stresses that a decisive change in the human heart can and does occur under the prompting of grace and the guidance of the Holy Spirit.

In justification we are, through faith, forgiven our sin and restored to God's favor. This righting of relationships by God through Christ calls forth our faith and trust as we experience regeneration, by which we are made new creatures in Christ.

This process of justification and new birth is often referred to as conversion. Such a change may be sudden and dramatic, or gradual and cumulative. It marks a new beginning, yet it is part of an ongoing process. Christian experience as personal transformation always expresses itself as faith working by love.

Our Wesleyan theology also embraces the scriptural promise that we can expect to receive assurance of our present salvation as the Spirit "bears witness with our spirit that we are children of God."

Sanctification and Perfection—We hold that the wonder of God's acceptance and pardon does not end God's saving work, which continues to nurture our growth in grace. Through the power of the Holy Spirit, we are enabled to increase in the knowledge and love of God and in love for our neighbor.

New birth is the first step in this process of sanctification. Sanctifying grace draws us toward the gift of Christian perfection, which Wesley described as a heart "habitually filled with the love of God and neighbor" and as "having the mind of Christ and walking as he walked."

This gracious gift of God's power and love, the hope and expectation of the faithful, is neither warranted by our efforts nor limited by our frailties.

Faith and Good Works—We see God's grace and human activity working together in the relationship of faith and good works. God's grace calls forth human response and discipline.

Faith is the only response essential for salvation. However, the General Rules remind us that salvation evidences itself in good works. For Wesley, even repentance should be accompanied by "fruits meet for repentance," or works of piety and mercy.

Both faith and good works belong within an all-encompassing theology of grace, since they stem from God's gracious love "shed abroad in our hearts by the Holy Spirit."

Mission and Service—We insist that personal salvation always involves Christian mission and service to the world. By joining heart and hand, we assert that personal religion, evangelical witness, and Christian social action are reciprocal and mutually reinforcing.

Scriptural holiness entails more than personal piety; love of God is always linked with love of neighbor, a passion for justice, and renewal in the life of the world.

The General Rules represent one traditional expression of the intrinsic relationship between Christian life and thought as understood within the Wesleyan tradition. Theology is the servant of piety, which in turn is the ground of social conscience and the impetus for social action and global interaction, always in the empowering context of the reign of God.

Nurture and Mission of the Church—Finally, we emphasize the nurturing and serving function of Christian fellowship in the Church. The personal experience of faith is nourished by the worshiping community.

For Wesley there is no religion but social religion, no holiness but social holiness. The communal forms of faith in the Wesleyan tradition not only promote personal growth; they also equip and mobilize us for mission and service to the world.

The outreach of the church springs from the working of the Spirit. As United Methodists, we respond to that working through a connectional polity based upon mutual responsiveness and accountability. Connectional ties bind us together in faith and service in our global witness, enabling faith to become active in love and intensifying our desire for peace and justice in the world.

Our Doctrinal Heritage as United Methodists

Theological Guidelines:
Sources and Criteria
(Doctrinal Standards and Our Theological Task,
Section 4 – Our Theological Task, Para. 63,
pages 74-75)

As United Methodists, we have an obligation to bear a faithful Christian witness to Jesus Christ, the living reality at the center of the Church's life and witness. To fulfill this obligation, we reflect critically on our biblical and theological inheritance, striving to express faithfully the witness we make in our own time.

Two considerations are central to this endeavor: the sources from which we derive our theological affirmations and the criteria by which we assess the adequacy of our understanding and witness.

Wesley believed that the living core of the Christian faith was revealed in Scripture, illumined by tradition, vivified in personal experience, and confirmed by reason.

17

Scripture is primary, revealing the Word of God "so far as it is necessary for our salvation." Therefore, our theological task, in both its critical and constructive aspects, focuses on disciplined study of the Bible.

To aid his study of the Bible and deepen his understanding of faith, Wesley drew on Christian tradition, in particular the Patristic writings, the ecumenical creeds, the teachings of the Reformers, and the literature of contemporary spirituality.

Thus, tradition provides both a source and a measure of authentic Christian witness, though its authority derives from its faithfulness to the biblical message.

The Christian witness, even when grounded in Scripture and mediated by tradition, is ineffectual unless understood and appropriated by the individual. To become our witness, it must make sense in terms of our own reason and experience.

For Wesley, a cogent account of the Christian faith required the use of reason, both to understand Scripture and to relate the biblical message to wider fields of knowledge. He looked for confirmations of the biblical witness in human experience, especially the experiences of regeneration and sanctification, but also in the "common sense" knowledge of everyday experience.

The interaction of these sources and criteria in Wesley's own theology furnishes a guide for our continuing theological task as United Methodists. In that task, Scripture, as the constitutive witness to the wellsprings of our faith, occupies a place of primary authority among these theological sources.

In practice, theological reflection may also find its point of departure in tradition, experience, or rational analysis. What matters most is that all four guidelines be brought to bear in faithful, serious, theological consideration. Insights arising from serious study of the Scriptures and tradition enrich contemporary experience. Imaginative and critical thought enables us to understand better the Bible and our common Christian history.

Scripture

United Methodists share with other
Christians the conviction that Scripture is
the primary source and criterion for Christian doctrine. Through Scripture the
living Christ meets us in the experience
of redeeming grace. We are convinced
that Jesus Christ is the living Word of
God in our midst whom we trust in life
and death.

The biblical authors, illumined by the
Holy Spirit, bear witness that in Christ
the world is reconciled to God. The
Bible bears authentic testimony to God's
self-disclosure in the life, death, and resurrection of Jesus Christ as well as in God's
work of creation, in the pilgrimage of
Israel, and in the Holy Spirit's ongoing
activity in human history.

As we open our minds and hearts to
the Word of God through the words of
human beings inspired by the Holy Spirit,
faith is born and nourished, our understanding is deepened, and the possibilities

for transforming the world become apparent to us.

The Bible is sacred canon for Christian people, formally acknowledged as such by historic ecumenical councils of the Church. Our doctrinal standards identify as canonical thirty-nine books of the Old Testament and twenty-seven books of the New Testament.

Our standards affirm the Bible as the source of all that is "necessary" and "sufficient" unto salvation (Articles of Religion) and "is to be received through the Holy Spirit as the true rule and guide for faith and practice" (Confession of Faith). . . .

Tradition
(Doctrinal Standards and Our Theological Task, Section 4 – Our Theological Task, Para. 63, page 77-78)

The theological task does not start anew in each age or each person. Christianity does not leap from New Testament time to the present as though nothing were to be learned from the great cloud of witnesses in between. For centuries Christians have sought to interpret the truth of the gospel for their time. . . .

21

The story of the church reflects the most basic sense of tradition, the continuing activity of God's Spirit transforming human life. Tradition is the history of that continuing environment of grace in and by which all Christians live, God's self-giving love in Jesus Christ. As such, tradition transcends the story of particular traditions.

In this deeper sense of tradition, all Christians share a common history. Within that tradition, Christian tradition precedes Scripture, and yet Scripture comes to be the focal expression of the tradition. As United Methodists, we pursue our theological task in openness to the richness of both the form and power of tradition. . . .

Tradition acts as a measure of validity and propriety for a community's faith insofar as it represents a consensus of faith. The various traditions that presently make claims upon us may contain conflicting images and insights of truth and validity. We examine such conflicts in light of Scripture, reflecting critically upon the doctrinal stance of our Church.

It is by the discerning use of our standards and in openness to emerging forms of Christian identity that we attempt to maintain fidelity to the apostolic faith.

At the same time, we continue to draw on the broader Christian tradition as an expression of the history of divine grace within which Christians are able to recognize and welcome one another in love.

Experience
(Doctrinal Standards and Our Theological Task, Section 4 – Our Theological Task, Para. 63, pages 78-79)

In our theological task, we follow Wesley's practice of examining experience, both individual and corporate, for confirmations of the realities of God's grace attested in Scripture.

Our experience interacts with Scripture. We read Scripture in light of the conditions and events that help shape who we are, and we interpret our experience in terms of Scripture.

All religious experience affects all human experience; all human experience affects our understanding of religious experience.

On the personal level, experience is to the individual as tradition is to the church: It is the personal appropriation of God's forgiving and empowering grace. Experience authenticates in our own lives the truths revealed in Scripture and illumined in tradition, enabling us to claim the Christian witness as our own.

Wesley described faith and its assurance as "a sure trust and confidence" in the mercy of God through our Lord Jesus Christ, and a steadfast hope of all good things to be received at God's hand. Such assurance is God's gracious gift through the witness of the Holy Spirit.

This "new life in Christ" is what we as United Methodists mean when we speak of "Christian experience." Christian experience gives us new eyes to see the living truth in Scripture. It confirms the biblical message for our present. It illumines our understanding of God and creation and motivates us to make sensitive moral judgments. . . .

As a source for theological reflection, experience, like tradition, is richly varied, challenging our efforts to put into words the totality of the promises of the gospel.

We interpret experience in the light of scriptural norms, just as our experience informs our reading of the biblical message. In this respect, Scripture remains central in our efforts to be faithful in making our Christian witness.

Reason
(Doctrinal Standards and Our Theological Task, Section 4 – Our Theological Task, Para. 63, pages 79-80)

Although we recognize that God's revelation and our experiences of God's grace continually surpass the scope of human language and reason, we also believe that any disciplined theological work calls for the careful use of reason.

- By reason we read and interpret Scripture.
- By reason we determine whether our Christian witness is clear.
- By reason we ask questions of faith and seek to understand God's action and will.
- By reason we organize the understandings that compose our witness and render them internally coherent.

- By reason we test the congruence of our witness to the biblical testimony and to the traditions that mediate that testimony to us.
- By reason we relate our witness to the full range of human knowledge, experience, and service.

Since all truth is from God, efforts to discern the connections between revelation and reason, faith and science, grace and nature, are useful endeavors in developing credible and communicable doctrine. We seek nothing less than a total view of reality that is decisively informed by the promises and imperatives of the Christian gospel, though we know well that such an attempt will always be marred by the limits and distortions characteristic of human knowledge.

Nevertheless, by our quest for reasoned understandings of Christian faith we seek to grasp, express, and live out the gospel in a way that will commend itself to thoughtful persons who are seeking to know and follow God's ways.

In theological reflection, the resources of tradition, experience, and reason are integral to our study of Scripture without displacing Scripture's primacy for faith and practice. These four sources—each making distinctive contributions, yet all finally working together—guide our quest as United Methodists for a vital and appropriate Christian witness.

Social Principles

Preamble to the Social Principles
(Social Principles, Preamble, page 85)

We, the people called United
Methodists, affirm our faith in God our
Creator and Father, in Jesus Christ our
Savior, and in the Holy Spirit, our Guide
and Guard.

We acknowledge our complete depen-
dence upon God in birth, in life, in death,
and in life eternal. Secure in God's love,
we affirm the goodness of life and confess
our many sins against God's will for us as
we find it in Jesus Christ. We have not
always been faithful stewards of all that
has been committed to us by God the
Creator. We have been reluctant followers
of Jesus Christ in his mission to bring
all persons into a community of love.
Though called by the Holy Spirit to
become new creatures in Christ, we have
resisted the further call to become the
people of God in our dealings with each

other and the earth on which we live.

Grateful for God's forgiving love, in which we live and by which we are judged, and affirming our belief in the inestimable worth of each individual, we renew our commitment to become faithful witnesses to the gospel, not alone to the ends of earth, but also to the depths of our common life and work.

Our Social Creed

(Social Principles, Section VII. Our Social Creed, Para. 70, pages 105-06)

We believe in God, Creator of the world; and in Jesus Christ, the Redeemer of creation. We believe in the Holy Spirit, through whom we acknowledge God's gifts, and we repent of our sin in misusing these gifts to idolatrous ends.

We affirm the natural world as God's handiwork and dedicate ourselves to its preservation, enhancement, and faithful use by humankind.

We joyfully receive for ourselves and others the blessings of community, sexuality, marriage, and the family.

We commit ourselves to the rights of

men, women, children, youth, young adults, the aging, and people with disabilities; to improvement of the quality of life; and to the rights and dignity of racial, ethnic, and religious minorities.

We believe in the right and duty of persons to work for the glory of God and the good of themselves and others and in the protection of their welfare in so doing; in the rights to property as a trust from God, collective bargaining, and responsible consumption; and in the elimination of economic and social distress.

We dedicate ourselves to peace throughout the world, to the rule of justice and law among nations, and to individual freedom for all people of the world.

We believe in the present and final triumph of God's Word in human affairs and gladly accept our commission to manifest the life of the gospel in the world. Amen.

The Ministry of All Christians

The Churches
(The Ministry of All Christians, The Mission and Ministry of the Church, Section I. The Churches, Paras. 101-03, pages 107-08)

From the beginning, God has dealt with the human family through covenants: with Adam and Eve, Noah, Abraham, Sarah and Hagar, Moses; with Deborah, Ruth, and Jeremiah and other prophets. In each covenant, God offered the chosen people the blessings of providence and commanded of them obedience to the divine will and way, that through them all the world should be blessed (Genesis 18:18; 22:18). In the new covenant in Christ, yet another community of hope was called out and gathered up, with the same promise and condition renewed that all who believe and obey shall be saved and made ministers of Christ's righteousness. Our spiritual forebears stressed this biblical theme of covenant-making and

31

covenant-keeping as central in Christian experience.

The biblical story is marred by disregarded covenants and disrupted moral order, by sin and rebellion, with the resulting tragedies of alienation, oppression, and disorder. In the gospel of the new covenant, God in Christ has provided a new basis for reconciliation: justification by faith and birth into a new life in the Spirit. This gift, marked by growth toward wholeness of life, is revealed in Christ who came not to be served but to serve (Mark 10:45) and to give his life for the world. Christ freely took the nature of a servant, carrying this servanthood to its utmost limits (Philippians 2:7).

God's self-revelation in the life, death, and resurrection of Jesus Christ summons the church to ministry in the world through witness by word and deed in light of the church's mission. The visible church of Christ as a faithful community of persons affirms the worth of all humanity and the value of interrelationship in all of God's creation.

In the midst of a sinful world, through the grace of God, we are brought to

repentance and faith in Jesus Christ.
We become aware of the presence and
life-giving power of God's Holy Spirit.
We live in confident expectation of the
ultimate fulfillment of God's purpose.

We are called together for worship
and fellowship and for the upbuilding of
the Christian community. We advocate
and work for the unity of the Christian
church. We call persons into discipleship.

As servants of Christ we are sent into
the world to engage in the struggle for
justice and reconciliation. We seek to
reveal the love of God for men, women,
and children of all ethnic, racial, cultural,
and national backgrounds and to demon-
strate the healing power of the gospel
with those who suffer.

The Heart of Christian Ministry
*(The Ministry of All Christians, The Mission and
Ministry of the Church, Section II. The Heart of
Christian Ministry, Para 104, page 108)*

The heart of Christian ministry is
Christ's ministry of outreaching love.
Christian ministry is the expression of the
mind and mission of Christ by a commu-

nity of Christians that demonstrates a common life of gratitude and devotion, witness and service, celebration and discipleship. All Christians are called to this ministry of servanthood in the world to the glory of God and for human fulfillment. The forms of this ministry are diverse in locale, in interest, and in denominational accent, yet always catholic in spirit and outreach.

The Ministry of All Christians

(The Ministry of All Christians, The Mission and Ministry of the Church, Section III. The Ministry of All Christians, Paras. 105-07, pages 108-09)

The church as the community of the new covenant has participated in Christ's ministry of grace across the years and around the world. It stretches out to human needs wherever love and service may convey God's love and ours. The outreach of such ministries knows no limits. Beyond the diverse forms of ministry is this ultimate concern: that all persons will be brought into a saving relationship with God through Jesus Christ and be renewed after the image of their creator

(Colossians 3:10). This means that all Christians are called to minister wherever Christ would have them serve and witness in deeds and words that heal and free.

This ministry of all Christians in Christ's name and spirit is both a gift and a task. The gift is God's unmerited grace; the task is unstinting service. Entrance into the church is acknowledged in baptism and may include persons of all ages. In this sacrament the church claims God's promise, the seal of the Spirit (Ephesians 1:13). Baptism is followed by nurture and the consequent awareness by the baptized of the claim to ministry in Christ placed upon their lives by the church. Such a ministry is ratified in confirmation, where the pledges of baptism are accepted and renewed for life and mission. Entrance into and acceptance of ministry begin in a local church, but the impulse to minister always moves one beyond the congregation toward the whole human community. God's gifts are richly diverse for a variety of services; yet all have dignity and worth.

The people of God, who are the church made visible in the world, must convince the world of the reality of the

gospel or leave it unconvinced. There
can be no evasion or delegation of this
responsibility; the church is either faithful
as a witnessing and serving community, or
it loses its vitality and its impact on an
unbelieving world.

The Unity of Ministry in Christ
*(The Ministry of All Christians, The Mission and
Ministry of the Church, Section IV. The Unity of
Ministry in Christ, Para. 108, page 109)*

There is but one ministry in Christ,
but there are diverse gifts and evidences
of God's grace in the body of Christ
(Ephesians 4:4-16). The ministry of all
Christians is complementary. No ministry
is subservient to another. All United
Methodists are summoned and sent by
Christ to live and work together in mutual
interdependence and to be guided by the
Spirit into the truth that frees and the love
that reconciles.

The Journey of a Connectional People

(The Ministry of All Christians, The Mission and Ministry of the Church, Section V. The Journey of a Connectional People, Para. 109, page 109)

Connectionalism in the United Methodist tradition is multi-leveled, global in scope, and local in thrust. Our connectionalism is not merely a linking of one charge conference to another. It is rather a vital web of interactive relationships.

We are connected by sharing a common tradition of faith, including our Doctrinal Standards and General Rules (1 62); by sharing together a constitutional polity, including a leadership of general superintendency; by sharing a common mission, which we seek to carry out by working together in and through conferences that reflect the inclusive and missional character of our fellowship; by sharing a common ethos that characterizes our distinctive way of doing things.

Servant Ministry and Servant Leadership

(The Ministry of All Christians, The Mission and Ministry of the Church, Section VII. Servant Ministry and Servant Leadership, Paras. 110-11, page 110)

The ministry of all Christians consists of service for the mission of God in the world. The mission of God is best expressed in the prayer that Jesus taught his first disciples: Thy kingdom come; thy will be done, on earth as in heaven. All Christians, therefore, are to live in active expectancy: faithful in service of God and their neighbor; faithful in waiting for the fulfillment of God's universal love, justice, and peace on earth as in heaven.

Pending this time of fulfillment, the ministry of all Christians is shaped by the teachings of Jesus. The handing on of these teachings is entrusted to leaders who are gifted and called by God to appointed offices in the church: some apostles, some prophets, some evangelists, some pastors and teachers, to equip the saints for the work of ministry, for building up the body of Christ (Ephesians 4:11-12). For these persons to lead the church effectively, they must embody the teachings of Jesus in servant ministries and servant leadership. Through these ministries and leadership, congregations of the church are faithfully engaged in the forming of Christian disciples and vitally involved in the mission of God in the world.

The United Methodist Church has traditionally recognized these gifts and callings in the ordained offices of elder and deacon. The United Methodist tradition has recognized that laypersons as well as ordained persons are gifted and called by God to lead the Church. The servant leadership of these persons is essential to the mission and ministry of congregations. They help to form Christian disciples in covenant community within the local congregation through spiritual formation and guidance for Christian living in the world.

Servant Ministry

(The Ministry of All Christians, The Mission and Ministry of the Church, Section VII. Servant Ministry, Paras. 112-14, pages 110-11)

CHRISTIAN DISCIPLESHIP—The ministry of all Christians consists of privilege and obligation. The privilege is a relationship with God that is deeply spiritual. The obligation is to respond to God's call to holy living in the world. In the United Methodist tradition these two dimensions of Christian discipleship are wholly inter-dependent.

OUR RELATIONSHIP WITH GOD: PRIVILEGE— Christians experience growth and transition in their spiritual life just as in their physical and emotional lives. While this growth is always a work of grace, it does not occur uniformly. Spiritual growth in Christ is a dynamic process marked by awakening, birth, growth, and maturation. This process requires careful and inten-tional nurture for the disciple to reach perfection in the Christian life. There are stages of spiritual growth and transition: Christian beginnings; Christian birth;

Christian growth; and Christian maturity. These require careful and intentional nurture for the disciple to come to maturity in the Christian life and to engage fully in the ministry of all Christians.

OUR RELATIONSHIP WITH CHRIST IN THE WORLD: OBLIGATION—The ministry of all Christians in the United Methodist tradition has always been energized by deep religious experience, with emphasis on how ministry relates to our obligation to Jesus Christ. The early Methodists developed a way of life that fostered reliability, and their methodical discipleship is best expressed in the General Rules that John Wesley first published in 1743, which remain in the United Methodist *Book of Discipline*, pages 69-72.

Servant Leadership
(The Ministry of All Christians, The Mission and Ministry of the Church, Section VII. Servant Leadership, Paras, 115-16, pages 111-12)

Within The United Methodist Church, there are those called to servant leadership, lay and ordained. Such callings are evidenced by special gifts, evidence of God's grace, and promise of usefulness. God's call to servant leadership is inward as it comes to the individual and outward through the discernment and validation of the Church. The privilege of servant leadership in the Church is the call to share in the preparation of congregations and the whole Church for the mission of God in the world. The obligation of servant leadership is the forming of Christian disciples in the covenant community of the congregation. This involves discerning and nurturing the spiritual relationship with God that is the privilege of all servant ministers. It also involves instructing and guiding Christian disciples in their witness to Jesus Christ in the world through acts of worship, devotion, compassion, and justice under the guidance of the Holy Spirit. John Wesley described this as "watching over one another in love."

ORDAINED MINISTRY—Ordained ministers are called by God to a lifetime of servant leadership in specialized ministries among the people of God. Ordained ministers

are called to interpret to the Church the needs, concerns, and hopes of the world and the promise of God for creation. Within these specialized ministries, deacons are called to ministries of Word and Service, and elders are called to ministries of Service, Word, Sacrament, and Order (¶ 323) as well as to the office and responsibilities of a deacon. Through these distinctive functions ordained ministers devote themselves wholly to the work of the Church and to the upbuilding of the ministry of all Christians. They do this through the careful study of Scripture and its faithful interpretation; through effective proclamation of the gospel and responsible administration of the sacraments; through diligent pastoral leadership of their congregations for fruitful discipleship; and by following the guidance of the Holy Spirit in witnessing beyond the congregation in the local community and to the ends of the earth.

The ordained ministry is defined by its faithful commitment to servant leadership following the example of Jesus Christ, by its passion for the hallowing of life, and by its concern to link all local ministries with the widest boundaries of the Christian community.

Called to Inclusiveness

(The Ministry of All Christians, The Mission and Ministry of the Church, Section IX. Called to Inclusiveness, Para. 117, page 112)

We recognize that God made all creation and saw that it was good. As a diverse people of God who bring special gifts and evidences of God's grace to the unity of the Church and to society, we are called to be faithful to the example of Jesus' ministry to all persons.

Inclusiveness means openness, acceptance, and support that enables all persons to participate in the life of the Church, the community, and the world. Thus, inclusiveness denies every semblance of discrimination.

The mark of an inclusive society is one in which all persons are open, welcoming, fully accepting, and supporting of all other persons, enabling them to participate fully in the life of the church, the community, and the world. A further mark of inclusiveness is the setting of church activities in facilities accessible to persons with disabilities.

In The United Methodist Church inclusiveness means the freedom for the total involvement of all persons who meet the requirements of The United Methodist *Book of Discipline* in the membership and leadership of the Church at any level and in every place.

The Local Church

The Church and Pastoral Charge
(Organization and Administration, The Local Church, Section I, The Church and Pastoral Charge, pages 114-15)

The Mission
The mission of the Church is to make disciples of Jesus Christ. Local churches provide the most significant arena through which disciple-making occurs.

Rationale for Our Mission
The mission of the Church is to make disciples of Jesus Christ by proclaiming the good news of God's grace and thus seeking the fulfillment of God's reign and realm in the world. The fulfillment of God's reign and realm in the world is the vision Scripture holds before us.

Jesus' words in Matthew 28:19-20 provide the Church with our mission: "Go therefore and make disciples of all nations, baptizing them in the name of the Father and of the Son and of the Holy Spirit, and teaching them to obey everything that I have commanded you." This mission is our grace-filled response to the Reign of God in the world announced by Jesus. God's grace is active everywhere, at all times, carrying out this purpose as revealed in the Bible. It is expressed in God's covenant with Abraham and Sarah, in the Exodus of Israel from Egypt, and in the ministry of the prophets. It is fully embodied in the life, death, and resurrection of Jesus Christ. It is experienced in the ongoing creation of a new people by the Holy Spirit.

John Wesley, Phillip Otterbein, Jacob Albright, and our other spiritual forebears understood this mission in this way. Whenever United Methodism has had a clear sense of mission, God has used our Church to save persons, heal relationships, transform social structures, and spread scriptural holiness, thereby changing the world. In order to be truly alive, we embrace Jesus' mandate to make disciples of all peoples.

The Process for Carrying Out Our Mission
We make disciples as we:

- proclaim the gospel;
- seek, welcome, and gather persons into the body of Christ;
- lead persons to commit their lives to God through Jesus Christ;
- nurture persons in Christian living through worship, baptism, communion, Bible and other studies, prayer, and other means of grace;
- send persons into the world to live lovingly and justly as servants of Christ by healing the sick, feeding the hungry, caring for the stranger, freeing the oppressed, and working to have social structures consistent with the gospel; and
- continue the mission of seeking, welcoming, and gathering persons into the community of the body of Christ.

The Global Nature of Our Mission

(Organization and Administration, The Local Church, Section I, The Church and Pastoral Charge, Paras. 201-04, pages 115-16)

The Church seeks to fulfill its global mission through the Spirit-given servant ministries of all Christians, both lay and clergy. Faithfulness and effectiveness demand that all ministries in the Church be shaped by the mission of making disciples of Jesus Christ.

A local church is a community of true believers under the Lordship of Christ. It is the redemptive fellowship in which the Word of God is preached by persons divinely called and the sacraments are duly administered according to Christ's own appointment. Under the discipline of the Holy Spirit, the church exists for the maintenance of worship, the edification of believers, and the redemption of the world.

The church of Jesus Christ exists in and for the world. It is primarily at the level of the local church that the church encounters the world. The local church is a strategic base from which Christians move out to the structures of society. The function of the local church, under the guidance of the Holy Spirit, is to help people to personally know Jesus Christ and to live their daily lives in light of their relationship with God. Therefore, the local church is to minister to persons in the community where the church is located, to provide appropriate training and nurture to all, to cooperate in ministry with other local churches, to defend God's creation and live as an ecologically responsible community, and to participate in the worldwide mission of the church, as minimal expectations of an authentic church.

The local church is a connectional society of persons who have professed their faith in Christ, have been baptized, have assumed the vows of membership in The United Methodist Church, and are associated in fellowship as a local United Methodist church in order that they may hear the Word of God, receive the sacraments, praise and worship the triune God, and carry forward the work that Christ has committed to his church. Such a society of believers, being within The United

Methodist Church and subject to its *Discipline*, is also an inherent part of the church universal, which is composed of all who accept Jesus Christ as Lord and Savior, and which in the Apostles' Creed we declare to be the holy catholic church.

Each local church shall have a definite evangelistic, nurture, and witness responsibility for its members and the surrounding area and a missional outreach responsibility to the local and global community. It shall be responsible for ministering to all its members, wherever they live, and for persons who choose it as their church.

Church Membership
(Organization and Administration, The Local Church, Section V. Church Membership, Para. 214, page 122)

The United Methodist Church, a fellowship of believers, is as a church also an inherent part of the church universal, which is composed of all who accept Jesus Christ as Lord and Savior and which in the Apostles' Creed we declare to be the holy catholic church. Therefore, all persons shall be eligible to attend its worship

services, participate in its programs,
receive the sacraments, and be admitted as
baptized or professing members in any
local church in the connection. (In the
case of persons whose disabilities prevent
them from assuming the vows for baptized
or professing membership, their legal
guardian(s) or sponsor(s), themselves
members in full covenant relationship
with God and the Church, the community
of faith, may recite the appropriate vows
on their behalf.)

The Meaning of Membership

*(Organization and Administration, The Local
Church, Section V. Church Membership, The
Meaning of Membership, Paras. 217-20, pages
123-24)*

When persons unite with a local
United Methodist church, they, or, if
unable to answer for themselves, their
parent(s), legal guardian(s), sponsor(s) or
godparent(s), profess their faith in God,
the Father Almighty, maker of heaven and
earth; in Jesus Christ his only Son, and in
the Holy Spirit. Thus, they make known
their desire to live their daily lives as

disciples of Jesus Christ. They covenant together with God and with the members of the local church to keep the vows which are a part of the order of confirmation and reception into the Church:

1. To renounce the spiritual forces of wickedness, reject the evil powers of the world, and repent of their sin;
2. To accept the freedom and power God gives them to resist evil, injustice, and oppression;
3. To confess Jesus Christ as Savior, put their whole trust in his grace, and promise to serve him as their Lord;
4. To remain faithful members of Christ's holy church and serve as Christ's representatives in the world;
5. To be loyal to The United Methodist Church and do all in their power to strengthen its ministries;
6. To faithfully participate in its ministries by their prayers, their presence, their gifts, and their service;
7. To receive and profess the Christian faith as contained in the Scriptures of the Old and New Testaments.

Faithful membership in the local church is essential for personal growth and for developing a deeper commitment to the will and grace of God. As members involve themselves in private and public prayer, worship, the sacraments, study, Christian action, systematic giving, and holy discipline, they grow in their appreciation of Christ, understanding of God at work in history and the natural order, and an understanding of themselves.

Faithful discipleship includes the obligation to participate in the corporate life of the congregation with fellow members of the body of Christ. A member is bound in sacred covenant to shoulder the burdens, share the risks, and celebrate the joys of fellow members. A Christian is called to speak the truth in love, always ready to confront conflict in the spirit of forgiveness and reconciliation.

All members of Christ's universal church are called to share in the ministry which is committed to the whole church of Jesus Christ. Therefore, each member of The United Methodist Church is to be a servant of Christ on mission in the local and worldwide community. This servanthood is performed in family life, daily work, recreation and social activities, responsible citizenship, the stewardship of property and accumulated resources, the issues of corporate life, and all attitudes toward other persons. Participation in disciplined groups is an expected part of personal mission involvement. Each member is called upon to be a witness for Christ in the world, a light and leaven in society, and a reconciler in a culture of conflict. Each member is to identify with the agony and suffering of the world and to radiate and exemplify the Christ of hope. The standards of attitude and conduct set forth in the Social Principles (Part III) shall be considered as an essential resource for guiding each member of the Church in being a servant of Christ on mission.

For Additional Reading

A Brief History of The United Methodist Church.
Nashville, Tennessee, Discipleship
Resources, 1998. Order no. DR100. Available from Discipleship Resources: phone
(800) 685-4370, fax (770) 442-9742,
online: www.discipleshipresources.org.

*The Book of Discipline of The United Methodist
Church*, Nashville Tennessee: The United
Methodist Publishing House.

Carder, Kenneth L. *Living Our Beliefs.*
Nashville, Tennessee: Discipleship
Resources, 1996. Order no. DR169. Available from Discipleship Resources: phone
(800) 685-4370, fax (770) 442-9742,
online: www.discipleshipresources.org.

Custer, Chester E. *The United Methodist
Primer, Revised*, Nashville, Tennessee:
Discipleship Resources, 1996. Order no.
DR024. Available from Discipleship
Resources: phone (800) 685-4370, fax
(770) 442-9742,
online: www.discipleshipresources.org.

Dunnam, Maxie D. *Going on to Salvation:
A Study in the Wesleyan Tradition.* Nashville,

Tennessee: 1990. Order no. DR024. Available from Discipleship Resources: phone (800) 685-4370, fax (770) 442-9742, online: www.discipleshipresources.org.

Heitzenrater, Richard P. *Wesley and the People Called Methodists.* Nashville, Tennessee: Abingdon Press, 1995.

Koelher, George E. *The United Methodist Member's Handbook,* Nashville, Tennessee: Discipleship Resources, 1997. Order no. DR219. Available from Discipleship Resources: phone (800) 685-4370, fax (770) 442-9742, online: www.discipleshipresources.org.

Norwood, Frederick A. *The Story of American Methodism,* Nashville, Tennessee: Abingdon Press, 1995.

Thurston, Branson L. *The United Methodist Way.* Nashville, Tennessee: Discipleship Resources, 1998. Order no. DR215. Available from Discipleship Resources: phone (800) 685-4370, fax (770) 442-9742, online: www.discipleshipresources.org.

_____. *A Brief Introduction to The Book of Discipline,* Nashville, Tennessee: Discipleship Resources, 1998. Order no. DR243. Available from Discipleship Resources: phone (800) 685-4370, fax (770) 442-9742, online: www.discipleshipresources.org.